Where Is
Georgia?

Where Is Georgia?

by Jennifer Marino Walters

illustrated by Ted Hammond

Penguin Workshop

To Dan: Thank you for always giving me someone
to look up to—and for letting me steal your
room when you went off to Syracuse!—JMW

PENGUIN WORKSHOP
An imprint of Penguin Random House LLC
1745 Broadway, New York, NY 10019
penguinrandomhouse.com

Designed and Produced by Dinardo Design, LLC.

Library of Congress Cataloging-in-Publication Data is available.

First published in the United States of America by Penguin Workshop, 2025

Manufactured in the United States of America
CJKW

ISBN 9798217051526 (paperback)
10 9 8 7 6 5 4 3 2 1

ISBN 9798217051533 (library binding)
10 9 8 7 6 5 4 3 2 1

The authorized representative in the EU for product safety and compliance is
Penguin Random House Ireland, Morrison Chambers, 32 Nassau Street,
Dublin D02 YH68, Ireland, https://eu-contact.penguin.ie.

Contents

Where Is Georgia? 1

Georgia's Land, Environment, and Origins . . . 3

Growth and Development 13

The Civil Rights Movement 29

Today's State 36

Georgia at a Glance 46

Timelines 48

Bibliography 50

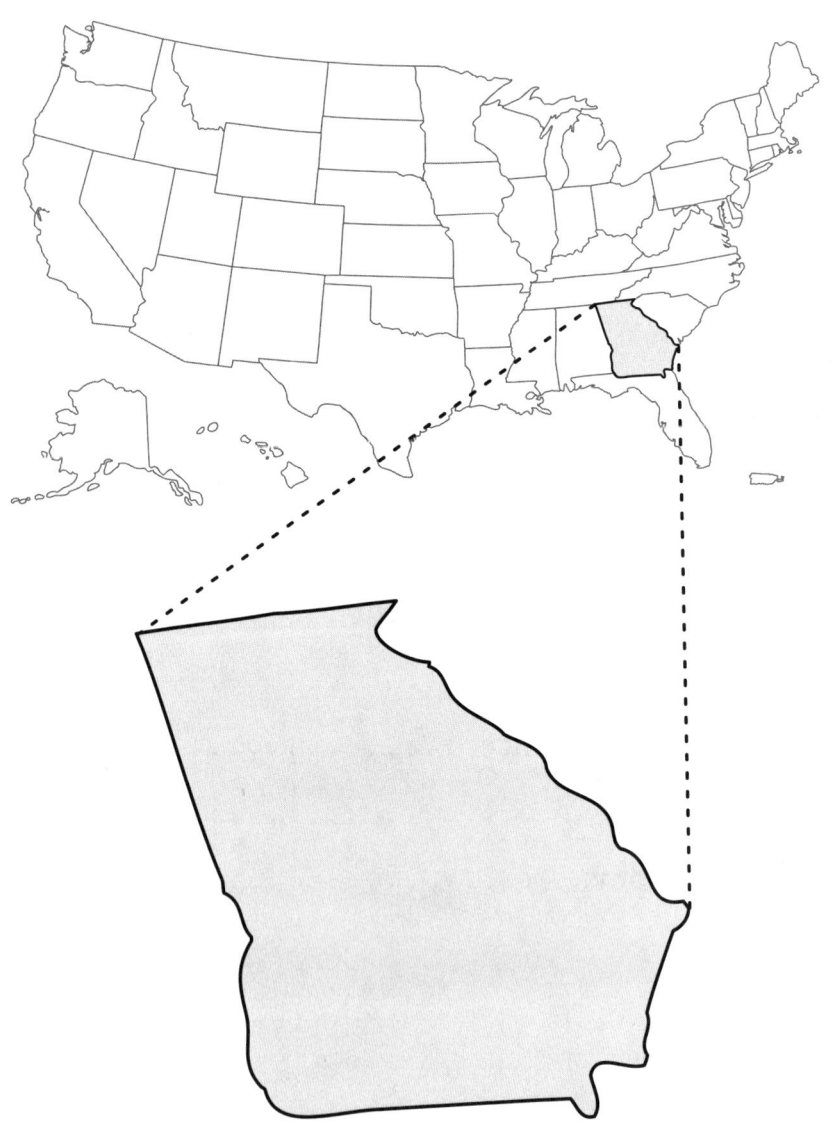

Where Is Georgia?

On August 30, 1961, Thomas Welch and Madelyn Nix walked into Brown High School in Atlanta, Georgia. Unlike most students returning for the fall, they were accompanied by police officers. At three other high schools across Atlanta, seven other students walked into classrooms with police by their sides. They were making history.

Welch, Nix, and the rest of the group, who would come to be known as the Atlanta Nine, were Black. Before that fall, Atlanta public schools had been all-white. At the time, segregation—the separation of Black and white people in public places like schools, buses, and public restrooms—was common in the US, especially in the Southern states. Black students in Georgia were forced to attend separate schools. Other Southern states tried to end segregation in schools. There was violence and protests from white citizens who didn't want Black and white students educated together. Atlanta mayor William B. Hartsfield wanted to make sure that violence would not break out in his city. He ordered police to be present at the four high schools on the first day in 1961.

Welch and Nix entered Brown High School without too much disruption and were able to leave at the end of the day. Some of their white classmates were friendly to them. Others did not accept them or were mean. But they and the rest of the Atlanta Nine had fairly peaceful first schooldays. They took the first step toward Atlanta school integration. It was a major advancement in the civil rights movement (the movement to get equal rights for all people regardless of race, sex, or religion) and a moment that the people of Georgia had been working toward for a long time.

CHAPTER 1
Georgia's Land, Environment, and Origins

Georgia is in the southeastern United States. It is bordered by Tennessee and North Carolina to the north, South Carolina and the Atlantic Ocean to the east, Florida to the south, and Alabama to the west. With a population of over eleven million as of 2023, Georgia is the eighth most populous US state.

Georgia's total land area is 59,425 square miles. That makes it the twenty-fourth-largest US state and the biggest state east of the Mississippi River by land area.

The Blue Ridge Mountains in northeastern Georgia include the highest point in Georgia, Brasstown Bald, at 4,784 feet tall. Thick forests in this mountain range are home to a variety of wildlife, including black bears, red-tailed hawks, and white-tailed deer. The Blue Ridge Mountains are also home to Tallulah Gorge, a spectacular canyon that's two miles long and nearly one thousand feet deep. The gorge was carved out over millions of years by the Tallulah River cutting through surrounding rock.

The Appalachian Plateau is in the northwest part of the state, which includes the 2,393-foot

Lookout Mountain, from which seven states can be seen at once! Also in northwest Georgia is the Ridge and Valley region, where many trees line the sides of steep ridges made of limestone, sandstone, shale, and other rocks that make up the earth.

In the center of the state is the Piedmont region, full of rolling hills, valleys, forests, rivers, and waterfalls. Most of Georgia's biggest cities are here, including Atlanta (the state capital),

Augusta (say: uh-GUS-tuh) (Georgia's largest city by land area), and Athens.

Georgia's Coastal Plain covers nearly the entire southern half of the state. This low-lying region is home to many marshes (areas of soft, wet land with many grasses and other plants) and swamps. Okefenokee (say: oh-kee-feh-NOH-kee) Swamp, which stretches from southeast Georgia into northern Florida, is the largest swamp in North America. It is seven hundred square miles—more than double the size of Augusta! *Okefenokee* is believed to be a word from the Creek language meaning "land of the trembling earth." Some of the swamp is covered with peat (the dark brown or blackish remains of plants that have partly rotted in water) that moves when the wind blows or when people or animals walk on it.

More than 90 percent of the Okefenokee Swamp is a national wildlife refuge. The animals and plants that live there are protected by the federal government. Alligators, otters, deer, hundreds of bird species, and many more animals live in the Okefenokee Swamp. Some of these species, like the eastern indigo snake, are endangered. There are also over six hundred species of plants. Visitors can take boat tours, ride the Okefenokee Railroad, and even walk into the swamp.

Georgia's Atlantic coast stretches for about one hundred miles. It includes over a dozen barrier islands. They are called barrier islands because they form a sort of buffer between the ocean and the mainland. They make for a protected, friendly home to marine animals like dolphins, sea turtles, manatees, and sea stars. The islands have gorgeous beaches, dunes, forests, wetlands, and reefs.

Tens of thousands of miles of rivers twist and turn their way through Georgia. The Chattahoochee River forms part of the border

between Georgia and Alabama and provides drinking water to half of the people living in Georgia. The Chattooga River flows through two other states, North Carolina and South Carolina. Because no cars or other motor vehicles are allowed within a quarter mile of the river, it is surrounded by forests and can be a very quiet place to visit.

Georgia has hot, humid summers and mild winters. Northern Georgia, near the mountains, is the coldest in winter (and sometimes even has snow). The Piedmont region experiences lots of thunderstorms. In summer and fall, tropical storms can bring heavy rains to Georgia. Hurricanes sometimes hit the state, including 2024's Hurricane Helene, which caused severe damage and killed over thirty people). Overall, the state's mild climate to enjoy outdoor activities like hiking, and boating all year long.

between Georgia and Alabama and provides drinking water to half of the people living in Georgia. The Chattooga River flows through two other states, North Carolina and South Carolina. Because no cars or other motor vehicles are allowed within a quarter mile of the river, it is surrounded by forests and can be a very quiet place to visit.

Georgia has hot, humid summers and mild winters. Northern Georgia, near the mountains, is the coldest in winter (and sometimes even has snow). The Piedmont region experiences lots of thunderstorms. In summer and fall, tropical storms can bring heavy rains to Georgia. Hurricanes sometimes hit the state (including 2024's Hurricane Helene, which caused severe damage and killed over thirty people). Overall, the state's mild climate allows people to enjoy outdoor activities like hiking, fishing, and boating all year long.

About two-thirds of Georgia is covered in forests, from the northern mountain regions all the way down to the Coastal Plain. These forests are home to about 250 species of trees. They include white and scrub pines and red oaks in the mountains, pecan trees in the south, and oaks and cypresses in the east. Georgia has more commercial forestland—forest that's used to make sellable products like lumber, or wood used for building—than any other state.

The first people arrived in the area now known as Georgia at least thirteen thousand years ago. These peoples were hunters who built small, temporary camps as they followed their prey. They lived in small groups of about twenty adults and children and hunted large mammals, including mastodons (huge, extinct animals related to elephants) and bison. The animals they hunted also provided antlers for tools, leather for shoes and clothing, and fur for coats.

In the period between 1000 BCE and 900 CE, the Woodland culture grew and included Indigenous nations like the Cherokee and the Choctaw. The Woodland culture is a name we use for a large group of peoples who shared some traditions. They built more permanent settlements because they began planting seeds to grow food. Woodland people lived in dome-shaped huts and built large mounds made of clay

and earth. Some of the mounds were human burial sites that also contained jewelry, pottery, and figurines. Others were made in the shapes of animals.

The Mississippian culture came after the Woodland culture and included groups of people such as the Guale (say: GWO-lay) and Creeks. The Mississippian people also grew their own food and built mounds that were used for ceremonies and as homes for leaders. Some of these mounds still exist today, including the six Etowah (say: ee-TOW-wuh) Mounds in northwest Georgia. These flat-topped mounds are now a registered National Historic Landmark that people can visit.

CHAPTER 2
Growth and Development

Around 1540, Spanish explorer Hernando de Soto led the first European voyage into present-day Georgia. The group was searching for gold and silver. They killed or enslaved hundreds of Mississippian people. They also brought diseases like smallpox, measles, and whooping cough that killed thousands more. After that, the Cherokee and the Creeks were the largest Indigenous groups that remained.

In the 1560s, the Spanish began setting up Roman Catholic missions (places to teach or do the work of the church) and presidios (say: pri-ZEE-dee-ohz) (military posts) on the barrier islands along Georgia's coast. They forced Indigenous people to live at the missions and convert to Christianity.

In the mid-1600s, the British in South Carolina wanted to expand their territory into Georgia. They began to damage the missions. Indigenous people also started attacking the missions. The Spanish were forced to close them. The last Spanish mission in Georgia closed in 1684, and the British slowly took over.

In 1732, an English soldier named James Edward Oglethorpe (say: oh-gull-thorp) wanted to form a colony where England's poor people could start a new life. He was granted a charter (a document stating that a city or town has been created) by King George II of Great Britain to settle on land that had been taken from the Indigenous peoples. Named after the king, Georgia became the last of the original thirteen British colonies.

Savannah, located in southeastern Georgia, was the state's first English settlement in 1733.

Oglethorpe was in charge. At the time, slavery was common throughout the British colonies. The British brought enslaved people from Africa to the colonies and forced them to work for free on farms and in their households as servants and to perform jobs like carpentry and sewing. Oglethorpe was against slavery. He banned slavery in Savannah and allowed religious freedom.

His plan was for the settlement to be made up of yeoman (say: YO-muhn) farmers (farmers who worked on their own farms to support their families) living in small villages and towns. Tomochichi (say: tow-mow-CHEE-chee), the leader of a small Yamacraw Nation (part of the Creek Nation), befriended Oglethorpe and helped him. A woman named Mary Musgrove played an important role in keeping the peace between the Creek Nation and the English colonists. She had an English father and a Creek mother, so she was able to speak both languages.

Still, Savannah was not as economically successful as Oglethorpe hoped it would be. Colonists were growing frustrated, and some began to move to other places. Control of Georgia was given to the British government in 1752. Small farms were replaced by large plantations. Georgia's plantations produced cotton, sugar,

rice, and indigo (a purplish-blue dye).

Large plantations like these existed in other European colonies in the Americas and the Caribbean. They relied on forced labor of enslaved African people, whose work created great wealth for plantation owners. By 1775, Georgia's enslaved population had grown from less than five hundred to about eighteen thousand people. People from African countries such as Sierra Leone, Angola, and the Gambia were kidnapped and sent to Georgia, where they were enslaved. The plantation system became the central part of Georgia's economy.

At first, colonists settled mainly along the Savannah River and Georgia's border with South Carolina. During the American Revolution (1775–1783), Georgia was a battleground between British forces from Florida and revolutionary forces from the North. Savannah, an important port city, was even under siege (with British forces inside the city and American revolutionary forces trying to regain control of it) for a month in 1779! After the British finally left Georgia in 1782, settlers began to move westward across the state. Georgia became the fourth US state in 1788 after it ratified (approved) the US Constitution.

though he was not violent, Dr. King was arrested several times.

The civil rights movement created change. In 1961, nine Black students began attending, and officially integrated, four previously all-white high schools in Atlanta. They became known as the Atlanta Nine. On August 28, 1963,

Dr. King led the famous March on Washington in Washington, DC. Over two hundred thousand people gathered in front of the Lincoln Memorial to protest racial discrimination and segregation and to demand equal rights for all people. That is when Dr. King delivered his famous "I Have a Dream" speech. He said, "I have a dream that my four little children will one day live in a nation where they will not be judged by the color of their skin but by the content of their character."

President Lyndon B. Johnson signed the Civil Rights Act in 1964, which prohibited discrimination based on race, color, religion, sex, and national origin. The following year, he signed the Voting Rights Act of 1965, which banned special requirements like poll taxes (money people were asked to pay in order to vote) and literacy tests that had blocked many Black people from voting.

Sadly, Dr. King was assassinated in Memphis,

Tennessee, in 1968. He is buried in Atlanta, and his grave is now a national historic site.

Today, about one-third of Georgia residents—over three million people—are Black. Georgia's residents celebrate many different traditions, including the Gullah culture, which was formed by enslaved people brought to Georgia and South Carolina from areas including West and Central Africa. The Gullah language blends English and African words, and Gullah customs such as weaving sweetgrass baskets are still practiced today.

Jimmy Carter (1924–2024)

Jimmy Carter (James Earl Carter Jr.) was born in Plains, Georgia, in 1924. His father was a farmer and businessman, and his mother was a nurse.

Carter graduated from the United States Naval Academy in 1946. When his father died in 1953, he left the navy and returned to Georgia to run the family's farms. He also dreamed of being in politics.

Carter was elected to the Georgia State Senate in 1962 and served two terms. He worked to change laws that made it harder for Black people to vote. He then served as governor of Georgia from 1971 to 1975. On the day he was sworn in, he said, "The time for racial discrimination is over." Carter helped increase the number of Black people working in the state government by 25 percent.

In 1976, Carter was elected president of the United States—the first president ever from Georgia. He served as president from 1977 to 1981. During his presidency, he continued to champion the rights of all people across the world. Jimmy Carter died in 2024 at the age of one hundred, making him the longest-lived president in US history. People can now visit the Jimmy Carter Presidential Library and Museum in Atlanta.

CHAPTER 4
Today's State

In the 1900s, Georgia shifted from a farming-based economy to one that relied more on service and manufacturing jobs, in part because farming was getting more expensive. Today, about 80 percent of jobs in Georgia are in services, including government, finance, construction, transportation, trade, real estate, and public utilities like electricity and gas.

Manufacturing accounts for a large portion of non-service jobs. Food and beverages, textiles, clothing, paper, chemicals, plastics, rubber, automobiles, transportation equipment, machinery, and electrical and electronic supplies are all big parts of Georgia's manufacturing industry. Georgia is one of the country's major producers of building stone, crushed stone, cement, sand, and gravel. It is also the largest producer of kaolin (say: KAY-uh-lin) clay in the United States. Kaolin clay is used to make paper and beauty products.

Many major companies—including Home Depot, UPS, and Delta Airlines—have their headquarters in Atlanta, where over five hundred thousand people live. Another major company headquartered in the city is Coca-Cola. In fact, Coca-Cola was invented in Atlanta. A man named John Pemberton invented the syrup for the drink and first sold it in 1886 at an Atlanta

John Pemberton

store called Jacobs' Pharmacy. It was marketed as a medicinal beverage, or good for your health. Carbonated water was added to the syrup to make a refreshing, fizzy drink. People went wild for Coca-Cola, which originally sold for only five cents per glass. Today, the Coca-Cola Company sells more than 1.9 billion servings of its drinks in over two hundred countries each day!

Though farming is now a small part of Georgia's economy, the state is still famous for some of its crops. Georgia produces over half of the country's peanuts—more than any other state. It is also the country's top producer of pecans. Vidalia onions are grown only in southern Georgia. Cotton, corn, squash, cabbage, and melons are other important crops.

Let's not forget the fruit that gave Georgia its nickname, the Peach State. Georgia is known for its fuzzy, sweet, juicy peaches. The Cherokee Nation first started growing peaches in Georgia in the mid-1700s. The Indian Blood peach had been brought to Mexico by the Spanish in the 1500s, and eventually it spread into the southeastern United States. Today, Georgia produces about 2.6 million bushels of peaches each year.

Millions of people visit Georgia yearly, drawn in part by its people's famously welcoming nature, known as Southern hospitality. In Atlanta, tourists can visit the largest aquarium in the western hemisphere, the Georgia Aquarium. There, more than five hundred species of fish and other sea creatures live in eleven million gallons of water. Atlanta is also home to the world's largest drive-in restaurant, The Varsity. It holds six hundred cars and can seat over eight hundred people inside. About thirty thousand people visit The Varsity each day.

Savannah is another popular tourist city. The charming city features cobblestone streets, oak trees dripping in Spanish moss (a flowering plant

that looks like long tangled strands), and horse-drawn carriages. The Savannah Historic District has original architecture from the eighteenth century. At Wormsloe Historic Site, visitors can witness the former plantation home of Noble Jones, one of Georgia's first English settlers.

Beach lovers flock to Georgia's barrier islands to enjoy sand, surf, and more. Driftwood Beach

Savannah Historic District

on Jekyll Island is covered with driftwood trees and branches. Blackbeard Island, named for the famous English pirate known as Blackbeard, is home to a national wildlife sanctuary and is only accessible by boat.

Georgia visitors can also explore many museums and cultural sites. In 2001, Atlanta's Fernbank Museum of Natural History became the first museum to display replicas of the world's largest dinosaurs in a permanent exhibition. Atlanta's High Museum of Art, Athens's Georgia Museum of Art, and Augusta's Morris Museum of Art are just a few of the state's major art museums.

Georgia is home to historic colleges and universities. The University of Georgia at Athens, chartered in 1785, was the first public university in the United States. Atlanta has two notable historically Black colleges—the all-men's Morehouse College (opened in 1867) and the all-women's Spelman College (opened in 1881). Dr. Martin Luther King Jr., director Spike Lee, and actor Samuel L. Jackson are among the famous Morehouse alumni (graduates). Dr. King's daughter Bernice King and author Alice Walker both graduated from Spelman. Georgia State University and the Georgia Institute of Technology in Atlanta are two other big-name colleges.

Various professional sports teams are based in Georgia. These include Major League Baseball's Atlanta Braves, the National Football League's Atlanta Falcons, the National Basketball Association's Atlanta Hawks, and Major League Soccer's Atlanta United FC. Augusta National Golf Club hosts the Masters Tournament each

year in April. Tournament winners are famously awarded a green jacket. And in 1996, Atlanta hosted the Summer Olympic Games. During the 1996 Olympics, the US women's gymnastics team won its first team gold medal ever, earning its members the nickname the Magnificent Seven. The twenty-two-acre Centennial Olympic Park in downtown Atlanta is a reminder of the 1996 Olympic Games.

Georgia has made a huge mark on American culture. Cable News Network (CNN), the first cable channel with twenty-four-hour television news coverage, started in Atlanta in 1980 and is still based there. Famous soul musician Ray Charles was born in Albany, Georgia. His 1960 rendition of the song "Georgia on My Mind" helped it to become the official state song. Other notable musicians from Georgia include rock and roll singer Little Richard and hip hop duo OutKast.

Some well-known authors have come from Georgia as well. In 1932, Atlanta native Margaret Mitchell wrote one of the most famous books of all time, a Civil War novel called *Gone with the Wind*. An author from Eatonton, Georgia, Alice Walker, wrote a novel in 1982 called *The Color Purple*. It is about the lives of Black women in the South and won a Pulitzer Prize before being made into movies and plays.

As one of the original thirteen colonies, Georgia was a founding member of the new country. It played a major role in the Civil War and in the civil rights movement, and it is an important cultural hub. From Mary Musgrove to Alice Walker, Georgia has played a large part in telling the story of America.

Georgia at a Glance

Statehood: 1788

Nickname: The Peach State

Abbreviation: GA

State Motto: Wisdom, Justice, and Moderation

State Tree: Live oak

State Animal: White-tailed deer

Capital: Atlanta

Size: 59,425 square miles

Population: Over 11 million

Famous People from Georgia:

Jackie Robinson (baseball player), Julia Roberts (actress), Ryan Seacrest (TV host), Trisha Yearwood (country singer), Halle Bailey (singer and actress)

State flag

State bird
Brown thrasher

State flower
Cherokee rose

FUN FACT:

The city of Albany, Georgia, has over 600,000 pecan trees! The National Pecan Festival takes place there each year.

Timeline of Georgia

1540 — Spanish explorer Hernando de Soto becomes the first European to visit the area that is now Georgia

1732 — Georgia is established as the thirteenth British colony

1788 — Georgia becomes the fourth US state

1793 — Eli Whitney invents the cotton gin in Georgia

1861 — Georgia secedes from the Union and joins the Confederacy

1868 — Atlanta becomes the capital of Georgia

1870 — Georgia rejoins the Union

1929 — Martin Luther King Jr. is born in Atlanta on January 15

1943 — Georgia becomes the first state to lower the voting age from twenty-one to eighteen

1961 — Nine Black students integrate all-white high schools in Atlanta for the first time

1976 — Georgia governor Jimmy Carter is elected president of the United States

1996 — Atlanta hosts the Summer Olympic Games

2024 — Hurricane Helene causes extensive damage in Georgia

Timeline of the World

1564 — William Shakespeare is born in England

1707 — England, Scotland, and Wales form the United Kingdom of Great Britain

1752 — Benjamin Franklin invents the lightning rod

1791 — The first ten amendments to the US Constitution, called the Bill of Rights, become law

1824 — Mexico becomes a republic three years after declaring independence from Spain

1867 — Alfred Nobel invents dynamite

1896 — The first modern Olympic Games take place in Athens, Greece

1928 — Bubble gum is invented

1937 — Amelia Earhart's plane disappears over the Pacific Ocean; she is never found

1975 — Bill Gates and Paul Allen found Microsoft

1994 — Nelson Mandela becomes the first Black president of South Africa

2024 — *Odysseus* becomes the first private spacecraft to land on the moon

Bibliography

*Books for young readers

*Boehm Jerome, Kate. *Georgia*. What's So Great About This State?
Charleston, SC: Arcadia Publishing, 2010.

*Kopp, Kathleen. *Regions and Rivers of Georgia*. Huntington
Beach, CA: Teacher Created Materials, 2016.

*Yomtov, Nel. *Georgia*. My United States. New York: Scholastic
Inc., 2018.

Websites

Atlanta History Center: atlantahistorycenter.com

Official Tourism Site of Georgia: exploregeorgia.org